I0839735

**Modelocity Online
March 2019**

Michael Herskowitz
Publisher

Belinda James
Editor-in-Chief

Angelo Ellerbee
Publicist, Double Xxposure

Aishaah Rasul
Attorney Counsel

Ronnie Walker
Art Director

Audrey Cain
*Executive Assistant to the
Editor in Chief*

Vin Taylor
Casting Couch Editor

Mary Coyne
Sports Fashion Editor

Ify Onwualu
Accessories Editor

Jill Foster
Beauty Editor

Emma Medeirus
Medeiros Fashion PR

**Celebrity/Contributing
Photographers**
*Blhackmoon Photography,
Mr. Don,
Hosea Johnson,
Finesse Levine,
Ronnie Wright,
Mr Chan Chui,
Shawn Montgomery,*

Contributing Writers
*Dorothea Trotter,
Shirley Smith*

**Entertainment
Correspondent**
Tuesdays Entertainment

Circulation
*www.ModelocityOnline.
com
Amazon.com
Magcloud.com*

PR Submissions
PR@modelocityonline.com

Photo submissions
*info@modelocityonline.
comPhoto releases must
be on file.*

**Ad Rates and Press
Information**
*Advertise@modelocityon-
line.com*

Vol. 3B

March 2019

*All rights reserved. This
publication may not be
reproduced without the
prior written permission of
Modelocity Online except
for a brief inclusion of
quotations in a review.*

*Modeocity Online Digital/
Print magazine available in
over 35 countries and
territories worldwide
published monthly.*

*Follow us on Instagram,
Facebook, LinkedIn and
Twitter @Modelocity*

THE EDITOR'S RUNWAY

Moving forward Modelocity Online will be the resource models, entertainers and anyone behind the scenes need to help them navigate through the networking events, fashion shows and other gatherings. You will need to be on your toes when it comes to conversations about the industry. Knowing your craft is one thing but knowing how your craft operates behind the scenes is a horse of a different color.

There will be many situations that may arise, and we want bells to go off in your head every time to alert you of danger or a great opportunity. 108 Rules of Modeling (available on Amazon) is a book every model should read to be aware of all thoughts and dilemmas that you may encounter on your career journey.

Next month we will start to reveal the photos of those who emailed their modeling photos for a chance to be featured in Modelocity Online magazine. Tear sheets are an important part of a model and entertainers' career. They show the world that you are making boss moves that puts you out in front of all the rest.

This is the only magazine that lets you talk to the editors regarding your career. Please take advantage of that opportunity because it will not be available for long. You can schedule appointments through Modelocityonline.com. When starting out, you will need all the advice you can get so that when you fall (and you will fall) you will know what to do when you get up. Falling is a part of your growth so don't be afraid to fall. When you do, Modelocity Online will be here to catch you.

Belinda James

Belinda Trotter-James is the creator and former editor in chief of Hype Hair magazine and other national fanzine publications with Word Up! publications

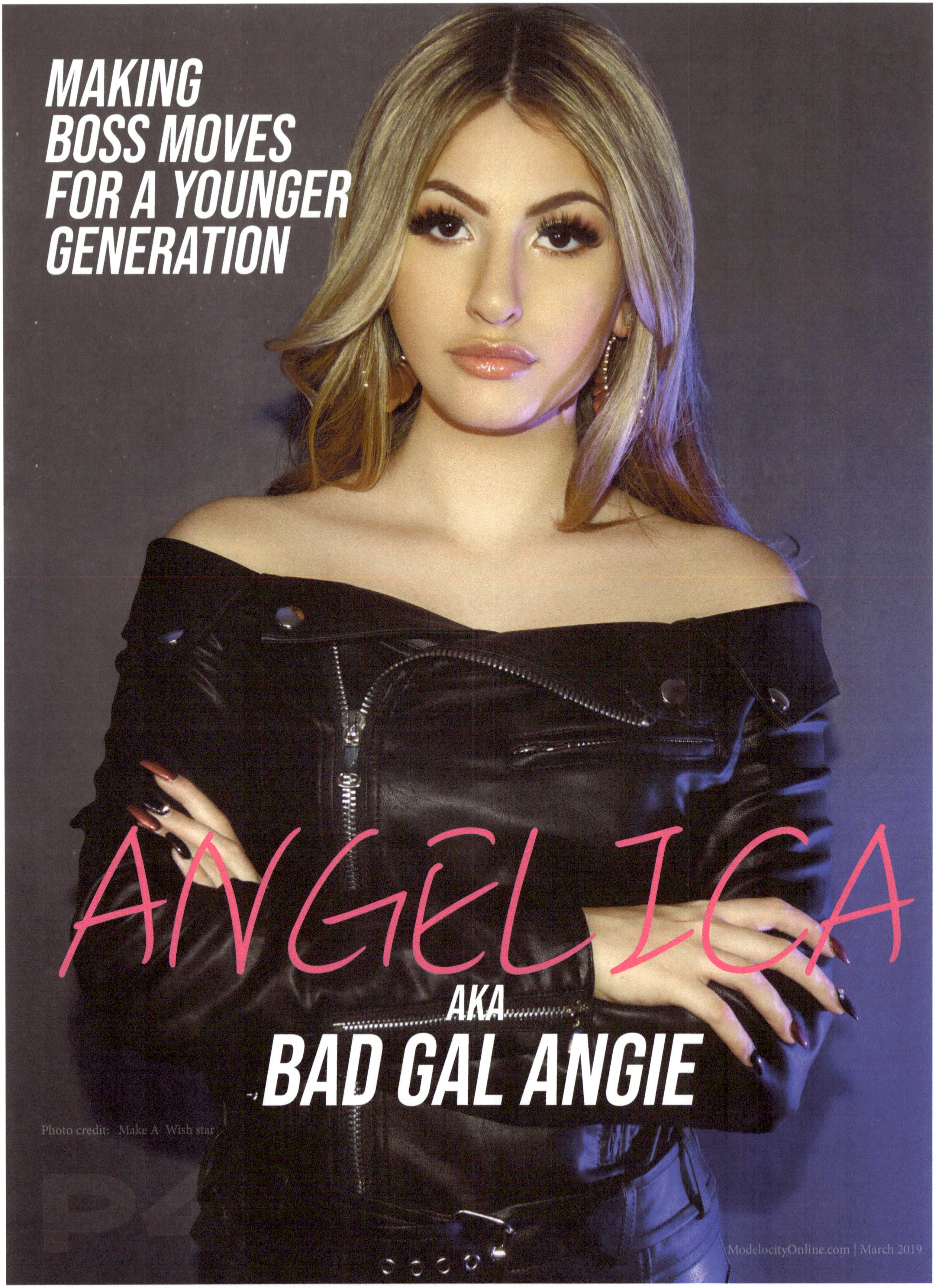

MAKING
BOSS MOVES
FOR A YOUNGER
GENERATION

ANGELICA
AKA
BAD GAL ANGIE

Photo credit: Make A Wish star

ModelocityOnline.com | March 2019

Named after her grandmother, Angelica is becoming one of the youngest large in charge artist in the music industry at the ripe old age of 14. She started making money while still in diapers by modeling for Neiman Marcus at 11 months old, began riding horses at two years old and has walked the runway at New York Fashion week. "I was doing a lot of things but did not discover my passion for music until I was 5 years old", remembers Angelica. "I joined the church choir and then my parents got me a vocal coach. I was only 11 years old when I started recording and released my first song, Rich Girl Mentality which received over 300,000 views. Within three weeks I got a call from Atlantic Records and when I met with them, they wanted to change my image by putting a grill in my mouth for an edgy look. That wasn't me", says Angelica. She did not take the deal they offered because she wanted to explore other options.

Pudgee tha phat Bastard, Angelica & Kal Dawson

Angelica continues, "Then when I met with Disney, they wanted to go in the opposite direction and put me in a rainbow skirt with a bow in my hair". AAAAAH!! What The…!!! We all laughed. "The third offer was with the UK. I got a song from Carla Marie Williams who wrote Freedom on Beyoncé's Lemonade album. I recorded the song and it was awesome, but I did not sign with the UK. Virgin Records came to my house and then some people from China flew in to meet with me and my parents as well," says Angelica.

After receiving a few offers, Angelica did not jump to sign with any of them. She decided to make boss moves with the help of her parents. Usually you cannot make it in the music industry without the power of a major record company to back up your career and take care of all the expenses. However, Angelica is proving that it can be done without a major record company backing you. It is a challenging road, but Angelica wanted to have full control of her music and image. She has been going full force for two years and everything seems to be dropping in her lap to the point that she can take time and select which deal is the best for her career. "Within the past two years, I had many offers but decided to pass on all of them because I want to have the freedom to say and be who I want," says Angelica. "I want kids to remember that if they decide they want to be in the music industry or do whatever they want to do, they have to be careful who they sign with and who they are going to be working with so that they can stay true to themselves and be what they want."

Angelic has been home schooled for 2 years and doesn't really miss the school setting because the private/prep schools she attended was so strict that they did not let the kids talk during lunch and socialize. Sheesh! How are kids supposed to develop social skills? The schools did not support her career when she would have to leave early for a meeting or gig. Homeschooling allows her to have the flexibility to work her career around her school schedule. Angelica does not feel she is missing out on her childhood by pursuing a music career because she can see her friends anytime she has free time in her schedule. "I think that when you love something, you have to make sacrifices," says Angelica

Angelica doesn't write her own music. She has two songwriters and a strong team of professionals behind her to make sure her career stays on track. Her angels seem to be working overtime because as soon as she entered the music industry, the doors just opened. She has not experienced pounding the pavement and having doors shut in her face. She dropped her first song and video at 11 years old and had record companies call her three weeks later. You rarely hear that type of story.

It can be very stressful to remember everything you have to do for a show, but Angelica has her own stress-free system. "I don't like when my people get freaked out the day of the show. I want to be completely relaxed," reveals Angelica. "On my way to the show in the car I listen to my songs that I'm performing. I don't sing along with them; I just listen to the beat and the words so that everything is fresh in my mind." She was blessed to have opened for the late Aretha Franklin in one of her last shows. What an honor to have had that opportunity to open for one of the greatest singers of all time. They call her the youngest in charge because she is touring with the big boys such as Fetty Wap, Fatboy, Tee Grizzly, 69, Funk Master Flex and Juju on the Beat just to name a few.

In ten years, Angelica will be 24 years old. Since she is so young, I just had to ask if she thought that far ahead in her career. "It's funny you asked that question because I was actually thinking about what I would be doing in five years," laughs Angelica. "In ten years, I can see myself doing a world tour, buying my dream house in LA, having millions of Instagram followers and at least 212 songs in my vault. Whatever it is, I will definitely be doing it in the music industry. There is definitely a million options for this question," says Angelica. Maybe venturing into the acting arena in a movie or TV show will be in her future as well. Her dream collaborations would be with Rihanna, Lil Baby, Post Malone and Lil Pump.

Fans can expect to have a great time dancing and jumping around to Angelica's music. It's a lot of upbeat pop tempos along with a club song, Good Girls Go Bad. "I have other songs that you can just vibe to and not jump around," states Angelica. "Dancing With The Stars is a calming song and shows off my voice. You can just listen to the words and enjoy."

It looks like being an independent artist is allowing her to navigate her career exactly as planned. Her father is a major supporter in her career along with Kal Dawson who oversees her media/press coverage, tour dates along with radio show interviews. Her mom is her manager who is a cross between Cookie from Empire and Kris Jenner all in one. "It's a challenging artist/manager relationship", says momager Lisa.

Angelica knows she has a lot of young fans who may also want to follow in her footsteps or pursue other dreams. Her advice is to do what makes you happy. "They must follow their dreams, work hard until they achieve what they want and don't let anyone tell you that you can't do it. Just make yourself happy and do it", advises Angelica.
No matter what you do, you cannot make it on your own. Angelica has an entire team behind her working diligently to make sure she is successful at every level.   You can follow Angelica and keep up with all her activities and promotions along with her thousands of fans on Instagram @angelicamusicxo and view her video on Youtube, Vevo and other media outlets.

BAD
GAL
ANGIE
Photo credit: Make A Wish star
ModelocityOnline.com | March 2019

THE CASTING COUCH

ARE YOU READY?

Vin Taylor

ARE YOUR SPIDEY SENSES WORKING WHEN IT COMES TO YOUR CHILD ACTOR/MODEL?

I could have made this article very short and said, "It is your responsibility as an adult to safeguard your child." But I think from experience that some adults don't understand what this means. That being said….

As always, the first thing I say about child actors or models is that they must want to be in the business. You cannot force your child to be your cash cow. As the parent or guardian of a child in the business, your eyes and ears must always be wide open. There are people working in the business that want to harm your child for their own benefit. You must not only checkout everyone that comes near them but be aware of all that goes on in their presence. Whenever an adult talks to your child, you must be in the room. Don't let anyone "talk" to them alone in a room. When there are any wardrobe fittings, costume or clothing changes, make sure you are present.

At auditions or photo shoots, you should be in the room. An agent, casting director or photographer should have no problem with you being in the room when any of these activities are going on. Also, talk to other parents or guardians at auditions or rehearsals to get their opinion on people or problems they have seen or heard with other people in the business.

Being the parent or guardian of a child model or actor doesn't give you the right to accuse someone of a career ending act when you have not seen or heard something with your own ears or eyes. You need to teach your child what is appropriate or inappropriate as far as when and if other adults or children touch each other. Do not jump to conclusions. Have it explained to you and understand what your child is to do in a scene when acting or posing at a shoot when modeling. You can talk to your child's agent and state whether you are comfortable or not with your child participating in certain scenes or doing certain poses that you are not happy with.

We live in a crazy day and age where unbelievable situations are coming into the light. You are your child's best defense. Although every situation will not be suspect; just be alert and make sure all your spidey senses are working.

NAME THAT MODEL FACE

In this industry you must know who's who. We have seen many aspiring models go into a modeling agency for an interview and not know the answers to basic questions regarding the fashion industry. Below we have the faces of some well-known models. See if you can guess who they are. The answers are at the bottom of this page. (No cheating!) You should also go to their pages to see how they became successful in a competitive industry. Getting inspired by other models and Modelocity Online magazine will help you stay motivated to make it to the top!

Answers:
1. Gigi Hadid 2. Eva Marcille 3. Chrissy Teigen 4. Alek Wek 5. Kendal Jenner 6. Naomi Campbell Photo credit: Wikipedia.org

WEARABLE TECHNOLOGY
NIKE'S ADAPT BB

By Mary Coyne

You knew it was just a matter of time: self-lacing sneakers. Nike has introduced the Adapt BB, the company's first crack at a "smart" shoe. Getting the right fit from a performance shoe is both personal and complicated and Nike feels it has found its most advanced fit solution to date.

Take the sport of basketball for example. Over the course of a basketball game, the foot can expand almost a half-size during play. So a level of fit that feels comfortable at one point might feel constrictive just minutes later. Because the needs of the foot can change at any given time based on the sport, its duration and on specific movements, the "perfect fit" is constantly changing.

Nike Creative Director of Innovation Eric Avar explains that because of the demands that athletes put on their shoes, basketball was picked as the first sport for Nike Adapt. "During a normal basketball game the athlete's foot changes and the ability to quickly change your fit by loosening your shoe to increase blood flow and then tighten again for performance is a key element that we believe will improve the athlete's experience," Avar said.

How does the shoe work? Using a power lacing system called Fit Adapt, users can adjust to find the perfect fit whether it's manually or digitally, using the Nike Adapt mobile app. A custom motor and gear train tighten or loosen to customize to your foot. Nike has added a personalization feature to allow fashion choices for its users. The two buttons at the bottom of the shoe light up in the color of your choice while programming them.

Priced at $350 the shoe is expected to be worn by professional athletes and Nike-backed college teams to start. Is this a glimpse of what the future of footwear could look like? I think so and while the shoe does not currently provide any data, it seems logical that it's moving in that direction.

Sports ~ Fashion ~ Technology …. What will they come up with next?

Visit my website for more articles, sports news and social media links. Mcsportbits.com

Strike An End Pose

Striking a pose at the end of the runway takes practice and exact timing. You can't be too far away from the photographers and you shouldn't be too close to the edge of the runway. No one wants to fall off the edge at a fashion show. You should know where the photographers are so that you can look into the camera and strike a fierce pose before the other model behind you gets to the end of the runway. No two models should be at the end of the runway at the same time. Photos that are fierce get shown on all the media outlets and the designers can't help but love all the media attention. Your stock will go up and you can become one of the "it" models overnight and sort after from every major designer. The models at the Diego Cortez fashion show by Angie Valentino at LA Fashion Week are masters of their craft.

Photo Credit: Blhack Moon Photography

Photo Credit: Blhack Moon Photography

To smile or not to smile is the question. It all depends on the instructions from the designer. If you are going to give a smile showing your teeth, practice in the mirror. You never want your photos to look like you're posing for a family portrait. Cheeeeezzze!

Blowing a kiss on the runway is not advised unless the designer wants that type of happy personality on the runway. Remember, anything that takes away from the garment is not recommended.

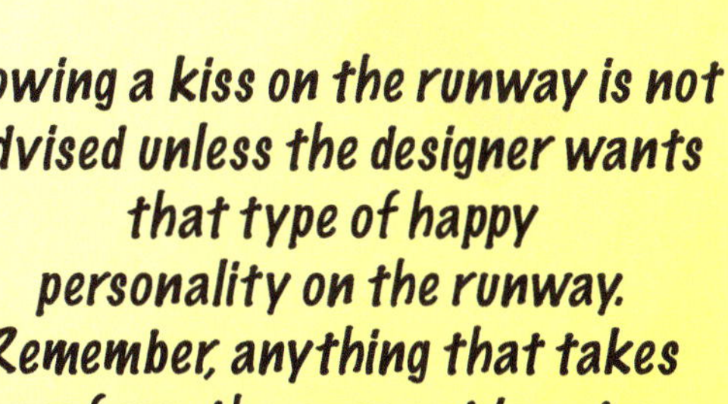

Photo Credit: Blhack Moon Photography

The side pose can be difficult because your body is facing one way while your neck is turned like something from the Exorcist. Your legs must be at a perfect angle and your facial expression must fit the mood of the garment and eyes must be able to find the photographer's lens

Photo Credit: Blhack Moon Photography

If you are going to touch your ear, commit to the pose and hold for two to three seconds. That should be long enough for the photographer to capture the perfect shot.

Photo Credit: Blhack Moon Photography

Posture is so important. The back must be straight or arched and chest out, chin up, arms at side, legs are anchored, and you are ready for the photographer to capture a moment in time on the runway.

WHAT YOUR JEWELRY SAY ABOUT YOU!

By Ify Onwualu, MBA

Jewelry is very personal, and it tells a vivid story about the person wearing it. Ergo, jewelry is the alpha and the omega of an ensemble. Therefore, what we choose to showcase is a determinant of how we're viewed by society. As a result, a true jewelry connoisseur can instantly decipher your mood, personality and some lifestyle choices, just by a brief observation of a simple piece. Likewise, the color scheme of your jewelry is another indicator of your feelings and what you're ultimately trying to convey.

Wearing elegant or classic jewelry pieces shows that you're perfectly poised in any setting. Therefore, if you prefer simple elegant pieces that go with everything, then it's very likely you have traditional values. Therefore, people find that you have classic taste in most things, which makes them appreciate your interesting yet understated personality. As a result, wearing diamonds is an indicator that you prefer jewelry that sparkles without the help of an Instagram filter. As well, wearing an engagement ring means that you like reminding your husband that there was a time when he spent copious amounts of money on you, lol. Likewise, people that only wear gold jewelry, prefer wearing their financial investments where they can see it (and so can you).

However, individuals that veer towards antique jewelry are typically nostalgic and bold trendsetters who are interesting and exceptional conversationalists. Also, it's pretty evident that you like jewelry that stands out and you appreciate wearing jewelry that has a story. This indivisible is known for unique silver pieces constructed from details that are remarkable yet stately. Oftentimes, antique jewelry wearers aren't usually not into brand names per say, however, they're very much into unique vintage items that are one of a kind.

Moreover, persons that prefer fashion jewelry are customarily fun, very colorful and yes...fleeting. Therefore, there's little commitment to their pieces, even though they may truly love them. This individual doesn't favor being held down but are more so free-spirits who don't stick to one era. In like fashion, shifting from style to style is accomplished with effortless ease.

Furthermore, individuals that wear simple and sophisticated jewelry tend to have an appreciation for a relaxed lifestyle that involves lots of trips to the beach and plenty of time with loved ones. Therefore, wearing thin, understated pieces that have pendants and small gemstones are ideal and are fashionably convenient since this individual doesn't prioritize sticking to trends. This individual doesn't have a preference between gold or silver, but rather something that shows them off without overwhelming them.

Conclusively! Now that you're privy to what your jewelry says about you and you now have a clearer understanding of how people perceive the pieces that you wear; it's possible that you may fit perfectly into one category or perhaps several. Ultimately, when it comes to Jewelry styles, everyone is as unique as the pieces they choose.

For further information contact:
Ify Onwualu, MBA, www.madisongems.com, Email: Ify@madisongems.com

WWW.IAMRONNIEWALKA.COM
RONNIE WALKA
NEW SINGLE AVAILABLE
THE STREET ALBUM
YOU AND I
AVAILABLE NOW
U & I

Available on
iTunes

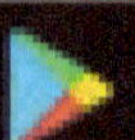

GET IT ON
Google Play

Know Your Industry Buzz Words

Check out each issue of Modelocity Online every month to learn new industry buzz words and terms to add to your vocabulary.

Fashion Photography Model: A model who is good at posing for photos that are used in advertising campaigns.

Fashion Print: A term used by models who may or may not have the height to walk a runway, but are good at posing and being photographed for fashion photos.

Fashion Show Season: The season when the new fashions will be shown on models in showrooms and on the runways around the world. Make sure you are with a modeling agency so that you can be booked for as many shows as possible in New York, Paris, Miami, London, and Milan for their Winter, Fall, Spring, and Summer collections.

Fashion Advertising Photographer: A photographer who shoots fashion photos for catalogs, billboards, department stores, magazines and newspapers.

MODEL LIBRARY

Front Row. She's ambitious, driven, insecure, needs, a perfectionist and considered the most poerful force in the fashion industry. She's Anna Wintour, editor in chief of Vogue, the world's fashion bible.

The Delusion of Cinderella. A young woman's obsession with her lover drives her into an emotionally destructive path.   She learns the hard way that Cinderella is a fairytale.

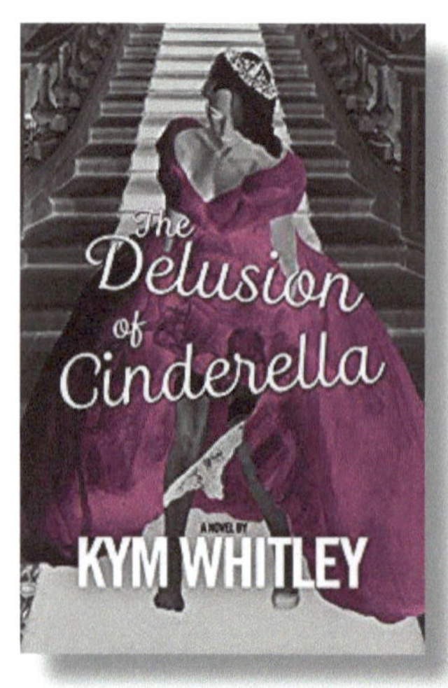

Becoming is the autobiographical memoir of former United States First Lady Michelle Obama. It's a must read for everyone who is curious to know who was Michelle before *becoming* First Lady.

#1 BEST SELLER FOR MODELS

108 Rules Of Modeling is the unlocked and revealed tips you need to crack the code to learn the rules of the modeling industry. This book is in bite size pieces to make it easy for you to remember the rules. If you are serious about your career as a model, it's a must have for every model and their parents. Exclusively on Amazon.com

#1 BEST SELLER FOR FULL FIGURED WOMEN

Power Of The Curves is the full figured guide to life, confidence and embracing your curves. The stories in this book from powerhouse plus size model/designer Jeannie Ferguson, comedian Luenell, actress Vivica A Fox and artist Rasheeda Wallace along with 16 full figured models reveal their most private thoughts of challenges and experiences. It's a must read for every plus size woman on the planet. Exclusively on Amazon.com

GLAMORY
AMORE 20
STRUMPFHOSE
TIGHTS
COLLANTS
GLAMORY
MY SIZE
ModelocityOnline.com | March 2019
P19

THINK COSTUMES ARE JUST FOR HALLOWEEN? THINK AGAIN!

By Emma Medeiros

Who doesn't love dressing up in costumes? Pretending to be someone, or someTHING, else has always fascinated people, especially in the ever-expanding world of "cosplay". Multi-award-winning cosplay veteran, professional plus model, licensed cosmetologist and makeup artist, stylist, entertainer, and costume designer GeishaVi dishes to Medeiros Fashion PR how empowering cosplay can be and why she's determined to make it more accessible to the many, many plus size men and women who wanted to join the community and couldn't because of costume size restrictions.

1. What exactly is a cosplayer and why did you want to become one?
We're creative individuals that enjoy recreating fashion, props and characters from TV, comics, manga, anime, movies and video games, often seen at conventions, parties, and music videos. I'd often imagine myself as a comic hero or villain as a kid and combined that with my love of fashion as I got older to create a truly unique form of artistic expression. Every new design is a puzzle that I love to solve!

2. Who is your favorite character to dress up as?
Definitely Starfire from DC's Teen Titans because she's usually portrayed as thinner, paler, and sexier than myself. Plus size girls were never encouraged to cosplay sexy characters. I do not feel the need to change who I am and, as a result, I've won multiple awards for my Starfire cosplay and people now always associate me with her.

3. What skills do you believe are necessary for a successful cosplayer?
Imagination to visualize, creativity to actualize the design, ingenuity to realize and craft it into being and, most of all, patience to keep a steady focused head while putting it all together! Everything else comes with practice and studying so don't worry if you aren't perfect at doing these things.

4. What did/do you find are the most challenging aspects of being a cosplayer, particularly a plus size one?
The combination of being plus size and being a part of multiple marginalized minority groups is very challenging; I've even been told that I should only do "black/ dark skinned/ fat" characters. This art form is limitless and by no means are there any rules that say you MUST have the same skin tone or body type as the original design.

5. What are some of the craziest reactions you've gotten from people?
The top of the top has got to be for my mermaid Queen Elunis; the gown is teal and silver with reversible sequins from head to tail and I was not ready for the amount of folks who would ask to pet my scales to see the colors change. They say it's very therapeutic for them. For me, it's a free massage of positive energy.

6. You're also an "alternative plus size model". How is that different from regular modeling?
Alternative fashion, more daring outfits for everyday or evening wear, has no restrictions on who can rock it. The "flaws" that would be considered a hindrance in regular modeling are embraced as pros, not cons, and the clothing is designed to fit my body type, not hide it or cut in away that looks/feels uncomfortable.

7. Why did you start designing cosplay costumes and what's your favorite costume so far?
I have a very eclectic style that's relatively new to America and is hard to find in plus sizes so I learned how to recreate the props, hairstyles and outfits of my favorite characters. My favorite costume so far is my mermaid Queen Elunis for which I learned how to make accessories with wire jewelry, shells, and reversible sequin fabric. NOT easy!

8. What cosplayers would you like to work with and why?

I'd love to work with SpazOutLoud, Fev Studios, Kelton Ching, Kamui and Cowbutt Crunchies, whose designs are stunning and functional while triumphing over technical crafting challenges. They're also free with advice, encouragement and motivation, which is so important in a community where everyone is always learning something new or improving a skill.

9. What are three weird/fun facts about you as a person that people may not know?

I'm really good at "quips", quick comebacks, learned from years of using humor to check people, especially bullies, for their rudeness. I enjoying teaching people with fun and understandable methods. I'm always professional whether I'm on stage or not, completely focused and totally dedicated.

10. Where do you see yourself in 5 years?

Joining forces with investors and sponsors to promote my company and creating more custom fashions, wigs and accessories in the cosplay, entertainment and fashion communities. As long as I'm accomplishing my goals while expanding my brand, I can help more people enjoy my art and embrace their courageousness!

To learn more about this curvy cosplayer, visit:http://geishavicci.wixsite.com/geishaviokiya
https://www.facebook.com/GeishaViCosplay,   https://twitter.com/goddessgeisha
https://www.instagram.com/GeishaVi/,   http://goddessgeishavi.tumblr.com/

About Medeiros Fashion PR: Medeiros Fashion PR is proud to represent a wide variety of plus size models, designers, photographers, retailers, bloggers, etc. We offer a wide variety of services (see the full list at http://www.medeirosfashionpr.com/services.html). To schedule your FREE consultation, contact emma@medeirosfashionpr.com.

BEAUTY BEHOLD BREAKDOWN WITH JILL FOSTER

5 Golden Steps for Cleansing the Face

Happy Saint Patrick's Day!!! It's the month of March, when the 'Luck of the Irish' take a day to celebrate themselves on Saint Pattie's Day! However, in the Beauty Behold World, the month of March is not only for the "Luck of the Irish!" That's right… You don't have to be Irish to strike a Pot-of-Gold! Beauty Behold Breakdown (BBB) provides you with golden facts and coins of luck every day starting with the common practice of how to acquire or maintain your most beautiful skin.

Outlined below are some golden facts along with golden coins for a daily face cleansing routine that will leave your skin fresh, supple, vibrant and looking younger than ever! BBB Golden Facts to Remember:

"Our skin ages more and more with each passing day, so adopting the below five simple steps will help aid against this and slowdown the aging process." ~BBB

"Our blood flow is higher at night which facilitates higher amounts of absorption of skincare product benefits that aid with minimizing acne, dry and flakey skincare issues." ~BBB

"Makeup and pollutants in the atmosphere can increase the size of our pores, so cleansing the face at night removes the makeup while also removing any excess oils (or sebum) and other pollutants that stretches out and clogs our pores otherwise." ~BBB

"Our skin temperature rises at night which can cause our skin to dry out causing moisture to evaporate, so using a daily face moisturizer after cleansing it aids in keeping the face hydrated." ~BBB

"Washing and treating our skin at night aids the skins natural process of recovering while sleeping. It facilitates the old skin cells to form at the surface layer, so repeating the process of cleansing our faces and repeating our skin care regimen in the morning, helps to wash away dead skin cells and the excess oils that occurs during the skin recovery process." ~BBB

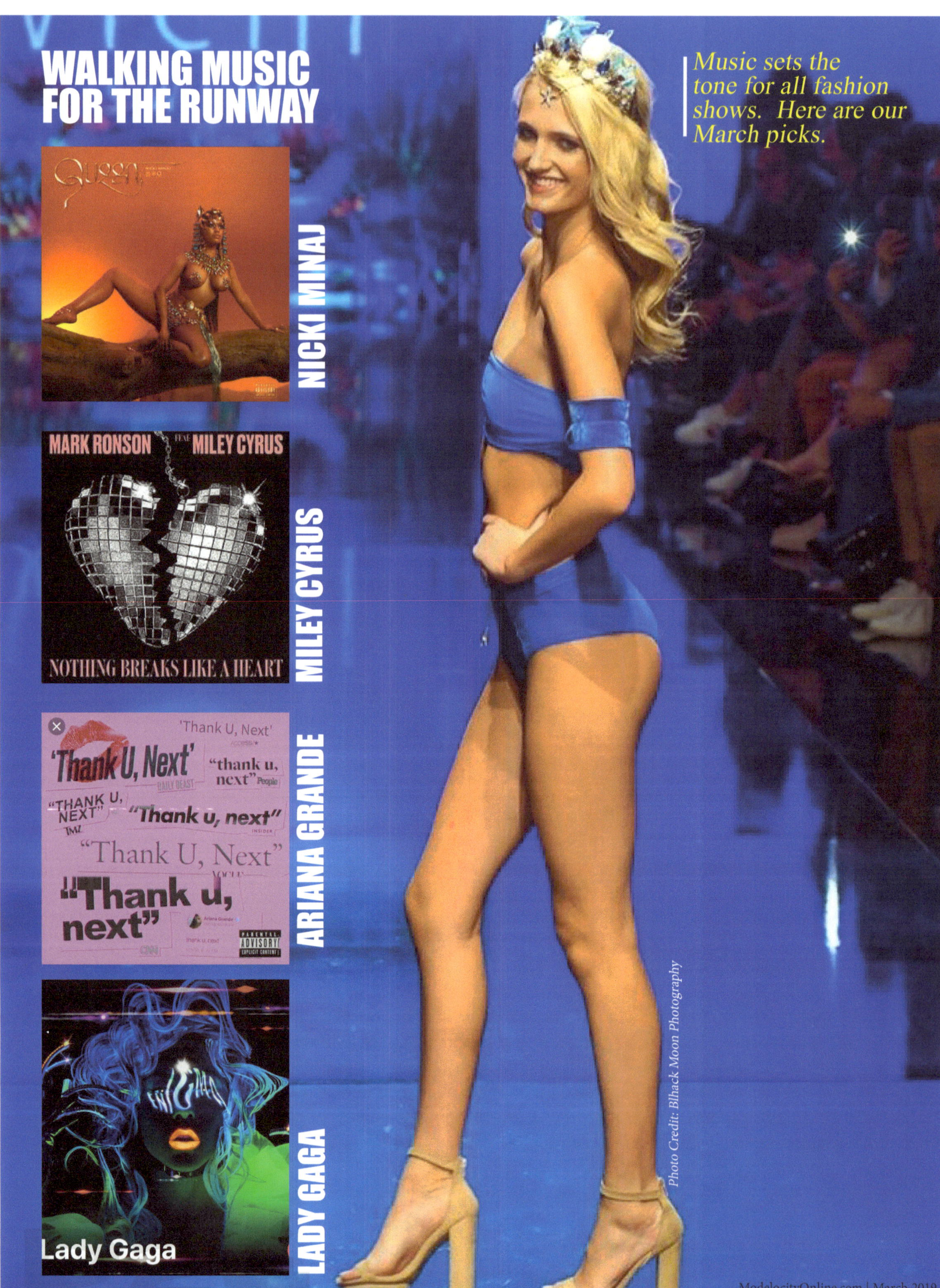

WALKING MUSIC FOR THE RUNWAY
Music sets the tone for all fashion shows. Here are our March picks.
NICKI MINAJ
MILEY CYRUS
ARIANA GRANDE
LADY GAGA
Photo Credit: Blhack Moon Photography
ModelocityOnline.com | March 2019

Cont from page 23

Keeping the above Golden Facts in mind, below are
5 Golding Coins to follow
as a daily skin care regimen.

Golden Coin #1
Cleanse your face twice a day BBB Recommended
Product Choice:
L'Oreal Paris Revitalift Bright Reveal Cleanser 5

Golden Coin #2
Tone your skin with a face toner
BBB Recommended Product Choice: Khiel's Calen-
dula Herbal-Extract Alcohol-Free Toner

Golden Coin #3
Apply an eye cream under the eye
BBB Recommended Product Choice: Reborneye
Eye Cream

Golden Coin #4
Apply a face serum
BBB Recommended Product Choice: L'Oreal Wom-
ens Revitalift Triple Power Serum Treatment

Golden Coin #5
Apply a face cream
BBB Recommended Product Choice: Day: Rénergie
Lift Multi-Action Lifting and Firming Cream - All
Skin Types; Night: Lancôme Bienfait Multi-Vital
Night Cream – All Skin Types

Recommended product choices above work well
with 'most skin types.'
However, it is encouraged that you
always check the labels of similar
products you may choose to use for your specific
skin type prior to use.

Email me with future BBB
subject matters of Interest.
Jill Foster, Owner / CEO
Beauty Behold LLC
www.BeautyBehold.com,
Jill.Foster@BeautyBehold.com,
(732) 588.7550

WORDS OF WISDOM

*Whenever you encounter a problem,
don't run into the situation without
first finding a quiet place to sit still.
In the silence you will be able to
hear a small voice with the solution
on how to move forward.*

P25

KAL DAWSON
MANAGEMENT

THE #1 MAGAZINE FOR MODELS IS HERE.

Modelocity online

Get your digital or print copy exclusively at www.ModelocityOnline.com

www.ingramcontent.com/pod-product-compliance
Lightning Source LLC
Chambersburg PA
CBHW040039240726
48664CB00003B/991